Exposing the Truth

Whistleblowing Uncovered

Exposing the Truth

Whistleblowing Uncovered

Learn the Secrets of Speaking-up

Exposing the Truth – Whistleblowing Uncovered is a comprehensive guide for those thinking of embarking on the whistleblowing journey, for those just starting on it, and for those who have come out the other side.

This book is dedicated to everyone who has helped make the world a better place.

Exposing the Truth

Whistleblowing Uncovered

First published in 2019.

ISBN 978-1-5272-4840-3

www.itrustassurance.co.uk

Exposing the Truth

Whistleblowing Uncovered

About the author

Nick Inge spent over 25 years in the police, nearly 20 of which were working in covert policing. He has managed people who have provided information about acts of criminality ranging from shoplifting to terrorism. He knows from personal experience what it takes to lift the lid on those committing wrongdoing and the journey that needs to be undertaken.

In an era of so-called 'fake-news', whistleblowing is becoming more commonplace as people seek the truth. It is therefore vital for whistle-blowers to be protected and for the recipients of information to be able to assess this accurately and without prejudice.

Using his extensive experience, he has founded a whistleblowing consultancy, iTrust Assurance Limited. iTrust Assurance Limited acts as an independent third-party that enables the voices of those with knowledge of wrongdoing to be heard in a safe and non-judgemental environment and aims to inform organisations in a supportive manner. It draws on many years of experience that include dealing with the most sensitive types of intelligence.

iTrust Assurance Limited offers a comprehensive range of whistle-blower-related services.

Nick welcomes questions and comments from readers. You can contact him via the iTrust Assurance Limited website www.itrustassurance.co.uk and via Twitter @itrustassure.

Introduction

Numerous books have been written about whistleblowing but this book is different. It is written by a whistle-blower who really knows what it takes to tell the truth, especially the truth about the wrongdoings of others. As you read this book, you will realise that it is authentic, factual, and not the work of someone who has studied the subject without any hands-on experience. By taking the advice provided in this book, what initially may seem to be a never-ending and gruelling journey will become a process that will make you a better person while improving the lives of others.

I began my career in covert policing in 1997 and have seen countless investigations initiated by people who have blown the whistle on those committing criminal acts. The value of whistle-blowers cannot be underestimated. Overtly and covertly, people will always provide information about others. You will therefore learn about the tactics needed to survive the process of whistleblowing. This will be of immense value to beginners, who will constitute the vast majority of readers, and those who have done it before and may identify with my experience. These are proven techniques that will guide people through the journey. They are tried, tested, and come from the heart. I implore you to use them just as I did in order to come out the other side. They are useful for those contemplating relatively low-level whistleblowing as well as those for whom whistleblowing will have far reaching implications.

It takes a few to stand up for the many. Although change sometimes starts in a small way, it can have a massive impact. Whistle-blowers must vow to do whatever it takes to reveal those who commit wrongdoing, for if they do not, it will continue. Go that one step further and, instead of moaning about wrongdoing, do something about it. Think back to a time where you wished someone had done something about it but did not. This is now YOUR time.

'Silence can be deafening but the truth is even louder'

This book has been written to inspire and empower you to speak up when you see things being covered up or people being wrongly accused in ways that are patently illegal or immoral. It is written to provide an insider's view of the process and the challenges to be overcome in a way that is free of complicated jargon or confusing statistics. The author has been there, done it and knows exactly how it feels to realise that something is wrong, the decisions that need to be made, and what happens both during and after blowing the whistle. He has spent nearly 20 years managing those that have faced the same dilemmas, often with spectacular results. This book seeks to help those who have witnessed dishonest behaviour deal with the stresses and strains of whistleblowing in a logical and straightforward manner. It stands both as a first-hand account of whistleblowing and a window into this world. It is based on the real-life experiences of hundreds of people who provided information on their friends, colleagues, and families and discussed the implications this has had for themselves and those around them. It offers an insight into the complicated decisions many of us wrestle with for the good of others and why this is important for us all. The narrative has deliberately been written to encourage everyone, regardless of where they find themselves, to build up the courage to speak out and be heard. For it takes courage, tenacity, and a clear sense of right and wrong to be able to follow this path. If this book encourages just one person to make a stand against injustice and, as a consequence, good comes out of that process, then it has been worth it. It is not intended to promote militancy, nor is it a rallying call to those who want to defeat the system - it is a book that will enable those who bear witness to wrongdoing to realise that they are not alone, that others have trodden the path before them and emerged as better people as a result. There are numerous examples throughout history that illustrate the ways in society has benefited from the efforts of those who are prepared to stand up and be counted, of those who stand up for integrity in a world where it is easier to turn a blind eye. This book describes this experience for those who may about to embark on that journey.

It can be used as a guide or as a reference book and will provide a reminder to all that this is no easy undertaking. Left to their own devices, wrongdoers continue to get away with all manner of ills. Unlike the silent majority, the whistle-blower will expose themselves to extreme scrutiny and invite forensic examination of their character and motivations. Hopefully, you will never find yourself in that position but, if you do, this book is written to guide you through the process. By reading the book, you will be in a much better position to survive the journey and empathise with those who are going through or have been through the journey. For the organisations this will have an impact on, it can provide the foundation for a change in ethos.

This, in turn, will promote a culture of openness that not only improves the way in which organisations operate; it will develop the trust and belief of all stakeholders.

'The biggest problem with liars is that they lie. Put it right. Expose the truth'

To blow the whistle is to report wrongdoing in whatever form it is found. Usually this occurs at work, although this is not always the case. On most occasions, it is carried out very carefully without revealing the person's details. Less commonly, it is done overtly; historically, however, such cases have been few and far between, primarily because of a fear of reprisals. The term "whistleblowing" is believed to have been created by Ralph Nader in the 1970s. Nader was a US-based civic activist who wanted to rid his nation of the stigma attached to those who reported wrongdoing by the use of terms such as "informer", "snitch", and "grass". These words are commonly used by those who consider such acts to be disloyal. More recently, the actions of whistle-blowers have increasingly led to changes in governments and in the behaviour of large corporations and have exposed the unlawful behaviour of high-profile individuals in the fields of commerce, entertainment, politics and sport. Nowadays, individuals have a certain amount of protection under the law. In the UK, The Public Interest Disclosure Act 1998 sets out the circumstances under which a person can make a disclosure that relates to wrongdoing. Nonetheless, the covert anonymous route is the one most people choose for their own well-being and protection. Although many people may want the truth to come out, they do not want to stick their head above the parapet because they fear the worst.

To protect society we use intelligence gathering in many different forms and this has continued to evolve over the centuries. As technology has improved, so has our reliance on ever more sophisticated methods of listening to chatter, both metaphorically and literally. However, none of this will ever replace the benefits of timely, detailed information from a source whose provenance can be established.

'Lies are like rotten teeth. One day they will come out'

Whistleblowing only hits the news when the story is unusual or the subject matter is likely to have a massive impact. For the vast majority of whistle-blowers, their concerns relate to their work and their surroundings. These are the everyday revelations that, to anyone outside the organisation, appear relatively trivial yet have a profound effect on those involved. For many, the concept of whistleblowing may sound daunting, terrifying, disloyal and, for some, difficult to accept. It puts people in a position that makes them vulnerable. Why, therefore, would anyone want to do it? What is the alternative?

This book will enable you to learn exactly what actions to take prior to, during, and after the whistleblowing journey. Although this will take you through a rollercoaster of emotions and many challenging situations, it will help you survive and come out the other side a better person.

A common response to those who have blown or will blow the whistle is "are you sure?" or "aren't you brave?" Well, it is not a case of being either of these – it is about doing the right thing and doing it in the interests of justice. Some may question your sanity as a whistle-blower. Some may think nothing has changed; the world has carried on. But has it? Those looking in from the outside might not fully understand the process, the emotions, and the outcomes. For those that do, they will see the whistle-blower as someone who possesses dignity, respect, and a sense of doing something rather than nothing. Doing nothing is the easy way. If every action was left to someone else, nothing would change, no-one would ever be challenged, and wrongdoers would be allowed to carry on. Although it is easy to understand how difficult it is for people to report wrongdoing, the fact remains that if nobody did, the world would be much worse off.

'The secret is that there is no secret'

This book has been written by a retired police officer who has been collecting information from whistle-blowers for nearly 20 years. This has been used to apprehend criminals and terrorists in countless operations. The benefits of this intelligence cannot be underestimated as the ripple effects of such acts, if left unchecked, can affect us all. You can easily be convinced not to provide such information. Listen to the advice but make your own mind up. There are many who will not say anything; yet, when the truth is exposed, they will suddenly start siding with those who were brave. It requires strength and resolve and provides you with a unique opportunity to make a difference. Take the initiative whilst others shy away.

There will be numerous reasons why you may try and convince yourself not to speak up. This book will help you understand the reasons why you should. This will not be an easy ride. The author will therefore guide you through the process on which you are about to embark and reassure you that you are doing it for the right reasons.

'Do not let others suffer in silence. Be the voice that they do not use'

Chapter 1

What Is It like To Blow The Whistle?

You may be wondering what it is like to be a whistle-blower. How does it feel and how would you do it? Would you do it overtly or covertly? What would happen if you got found out, or perhaps you do not mind everyone knowing what you have done? How would you like to be labelled as a "grass" or a "snitch" or someone who cannot be trusted with a secret?

But what if that secret could help a friend or colleague or someone you do not even know? What would be your reasons for revealing it? There are many - money, revenge, religion, hatred, jealousy, or simply a basic sense of what is right and wrong. And what if you were wrong – what would be the implications?

Whistleblowing at any level is not for the faint-hearted. It takes courage, resolve, passion, belief, faith and perseverance. It involves using every ounce of your integrity and the support from friends and family to do what you know is right. This all depends on your own morals, ethics, age, support network, and experience. And what will happen after you have told all? When is the exact time and moment you tell someone what you know? Will they believe you and will you be taken seriously? Will you become paranoid? Are you ready for any backlash? How will you cope and what will be the long-term effects?

Whistleblowing is becoming more accepted in society and for all the right reasons. By whistleblowing I'm not simply talking about tittle tattle, I'm talking about people providing information about bullying, harassment, corrupt practices, poor leadership, back-handers, and so forth. The established status quo is increasingly being challenged in a context where respected members of the community have been exposed for serious wrongdoing and corrupt practices have been outed. A domino effect can clearly be seen, which is all for the good.

'It's only the world that has gone mad, not you. Keep the faith. For you know the real truth'

If you have a strong belief in the truth and what is right, then whistleblowing is for you. Whistle-blowers are brave. It takes guts and a fundamental belief in justice to stand up and be counted. It is not easy, believe me. If the fabric of your soul would rather see right prevail over wrong, if you revile those who blatantly flout the rules and think they can get away with it, and condemn those who, because of their position, make the system work for themselves at the expense of others, then this could be for you. Why should others benefit from wrongdoing? Wrongdoing is the art of putting two fingers up to colleagues, teammates and society by those who think they are better than everyone else. In many instances, people who think like this try to intimidate others who they believe lack the strength to tell others what they know. Whistleblowing indeed takes strength, it takes courage and it takes conviction. It takes resolve and perseverance. It takes the support of family and friends and a belief that you are 100% correct in what you witness and then report.

There are many questions that you might ask yourself, or that might be asked of you if and when you report wrongdoing. What does it feel like to take that step from knowing about wrongdoing to telling someone you might not even know or fully trust? There may not be any obvious answers as you are likely to be in a unique position. However, simply knowing that the questions you may ask yourself have already been asked by others in a similar position should be of comfort to you.

Let no-one underestimate what it takes to tell someone else what you know - it is a massive step. You may have stored the knowledge you have gained about wrongdoing for a long period of time, the pressure building over weeks, months, and years; all bottled up just waiting for the metaphorical cork to be popped. It is taking that next step of popping the cork that may prove to be the biggest hurdle.

'Finding out about the truth can be easy. Telling the truth can be the tricky bit. Do the right thing'

Below are a few emotions you may experience and questions to which you may want answers. I have highlighted these as being the feelings you are most likely to experience:

Isolation

Telling the truth to someone about another person may make you feel terribly isolated, disloyal, angry, in despair, and vulnerable.

Why Me?

You may wonder how you ever found yourself in this position? You know that you went along with all the policies put in place to protect you and your colleagues, yet here you are. It feels like being on the outside looking in on someone else, only it is not. It is you.

Disapproval

People may approve, disapprove, support you, or not support you. Your family may be affected as well as your friends. You may think you are going mad. It is likely you will need counselling in the very early stages to help you come to terms with what you have done. Do not be afraid to take it if it is offered. I found it to be very beneficial.

Paranoia

You may feel paranoid – are those you reported watching you? What will be the consequences of telling the truth? Will there be any backlash?

Escape

It may feel easier just to run away, but this is not likely to be possible.

Sleeplessness

You may wake up in the night because you cannot get the situation out of your head.

Repetitive Thoughts

You may be constantly thinking about conversations and scenarios (past, present and future).

Information

You may obtain snippets of information from friends and colleagues which allow you to piece together your next move.

'Never devalue yourself. Your integrity is worth far more than their lies'

If you are anything like me, you may want any investigation into a disclosure you make to have started yesterday. You may ask yourself how long it takes to investigate and deal with wrongdoers? And will the truth ever come out? Will there ever be justice? Do you hope that the wrongdoers suffer like you have? You may want them to suffer even more.

All the good qualities you have as a person may disappear

as you want them to admit the truth (which they may) and, if they do not, suffer the full consequences. Will other colleagues who may have witnessed wrongdoing stand by you? It may be that whatever they say initially in support may evaporate as time passes and the wrongdoers curry favour with those left behind. Did you do the right thing?

One of the major problems you will encounter when faced with the dilemma of what to do concerns who to tell. Do you tell your friends, family, the wrongdoer, colleagues, or an anonymous whistleblowing hotline? Do you perhaps use the media? The first person you are likely to tell is your partner or a very close and trusted friend. They may have nothing to do with your work but are someone for you to offload upon. Someone you can trust who will listen and who will be sympathetic, someone to give you advice.

Is it worth your angst and worry compared with your anger and sense of justice, should any enquiry be successful? Is this to be weighed against the maximum punishment that could be brought against a wrongdoer?

Know what the process is before you embark on your journey. What do you want out of it? Ask yourself realistically what will happen. Will you be happy with the outcome of an investigation or is it simply enough to know that you have done your bit? You should also make sure that what you do is valid. It may well lead you to question your morals, your principles and your values, your sanity, and your religious beliefs.

With all these questions in your mind you may be thinking - what is the point? Nothing appears clear and there is no apparent right or wrong way of getting through this journey. My advice to you is this - look at yourself as a human being. If you can say with 100% certainty that you know what others have done is wrong and, regardless of the outcome, you can leave this planet knowing that you were honourable, true to your word, and courageous, then do it. Do not do it solely for the benefit of others. Do it so that you can look the wrongdoer in the eye and know that you are right and they are wrong. Once you have determined that this is where you are, the rest will fall into place.

'The sound of silence is music to their ears. Sing it out loud'

Chapter 2

How Hungry Are You?

To make this happen and see it through to the end you need an appetite: a massive appetite. A desire to let someone know what has happened and then stay the course. You will need a positive outlook, a motivation to ensure that the full facts emerge, and the stamina to see it through to the end.

'You are stronger than you imagine. Then imagine you are stronger than that. Go for it'

There are no half measures, no half-hearted attempts to sort of let someone know. You either do it or you do not. And why wouldn't this be the case? If you do something, you do it properly. You do it to the best of your ability and you ensure that whatever the outcome you gave it your best shot. This is not to say that you go over top in what you disclose. You do not become so passionate about what you have done that you attract ridicule. People will expect you to stay focused and determined. There is little point starting the process full of good intentions and then, within a few hours, days or weeks, changing your mind. Once the pistol is fired the race is underway. In this game there are no half measures. You are either in or you are not. You choose.

'Find your fire within. Reveal their deceit'

Desire

Desire is half the battle. If you think you can, you can. If you think you cannot, you will not. Believe in your ability to do what you know in your heart is right and that hunger has to come from deep in your soul. Only you know how hungry you are for the truth to be revealed. Only you know what this will mean for other people. Try to put yourself in their shoes. How hungry will they be for someone to have the courage to speak up on their behalf.

'If you want change, be the change'

Determination

The determination to reveal the truth doesn't just come from you. There are others who do not even know about the wrongdoing but will give you added determination once you have revealed it. So do not do it just for you, do it for others who have been directly affected as well as for a wider group of people who will want you to do this in the interests of morality, ethics, and justice. No-one wants to see those committing wrongdoing get away with it. Be the one who stands up and is counted.

'Take no nonsense. Speak up and be heard. The truth will prevail and so will you'

The Truth

The truth is that there is no secret. There is probably someone somewhere who also knows what you know. You may think that you are the only person who knows but I would suggest this is unlikely. Ask yourself this - is telling someone a secret because some form of wrongdoing has been committed better than not telling someone? If you have doubts, consult your organisations' policy, ask a friend or colleague, or consult your union or trade association. Do not just sit there and do nothing: this is far worse than doing something. If, in one week, one month, or even years down the line it comes to light that you have done nothing and are implicated in an investigation, you could be just as culpable as those involved in the wrongdoing.

'If you cannot get it out of your head get it into someone else's'

Do Something

If you decide not to act on what you know it will be on your conscience that you could have started an investigation into, for example, another bullying issue, an incident involving sexual harassment, a flagrant abuse of power or, in a worst case scenario, the death of a colleague or member of the public. Only you can make the decision to do something about what you know. You may be surprised to find that what you know is also known by a lot of your colleagues – it is just that they have never done anything about it.

'Ice in your head, fire in your belly, truth on your tongue'

Do the Right Thing

How many times throughout history have we seen the domino effect where something begun by just one person turns into an avalanche of claims that uncover wrongdoing on a massive scale. Mark Felt (Richard Nixon), and more recently Christopher Wylie (Facebook/Cambridge Analytica), are examples of how just one person can change the course of history for the better. Without these people the world would have been none the wiser and further cheating, wrongdoing, and deceit would have been carried out. Without whistle-blowers there would be unknown victims of sexual abuse, bullying, human trafficking, or breaches of data protection on an industrial scale - and those people would still be suffering.

'It just gets to the point when you just know. Stop the rot. Expose the truth'

Chapter 3

What Would Motivate You?

Why on earth would you want to provide information as a whistle-blower? What would impel you to speak up and provide information about others? The list of reasons as to why people provide information is infinitely long and highly personal to each and every person who does so. They are unique reasons based on that individual's experience, age, situation, and knowledge.

What have you done recently that you are proud of? Is it helping out a neighbour or guiding an elderly person across the road? It may be something different. Could you help a colleague who is being bullied at work by identifying and providing evidence against the bully to ensure your colleague no longer suffers? Could it be that, by revealing the truth, in years to come someone you helped at work with whom you are no longer in contact thinks of you and thanks you for your selfless act? The important fact is that you were motivated to stand up and be counted, instead of looking the other way and not doing anything. It is easy to do nothing, far more difficult to say something. The act of doing good with regard to whistleblowing is not an easy one and is something the vast majority of people would not do. It is generally carried out as a one off. Due to its very nature there are no professional whistle-blowers!

Therefore, if you decide to speak-up you will be part of a very small exclusive club. You will have the amazing feeling that you have changed someone's life by being brave. Only you can decide.

'See evil, feel evil, hear evil. Do not just sit there. Do something about it'

Listed below are the main reasons that drive people to provide information about others, both in a criminal and in a civil environment:

Moral

Everyone knows the difference between right and wrong. You know when something is right and when it is not. And everyone knows on a sliding scale where the boundaries are crossed. For example, if you are a passenger travelling in your boss's car, you would be very unlikely to report them for speeding if they went 5km/h over the limit; however, if they drove at 100km/h an hour that would probably be a completely different situation. Your reaction will depend on your relationship with that person, your position in the company, your age and experience, and your background (have you just had a speeding ticket?). The moral maze is very complicated and hazardous to navigate.

'It's easy to ignore the past but you only make the future more difficult'

Dislike

I know very few people in life who go through their working week without disliking someone. I'm not just talking about a mild dislike, I'm talking about a complete disdain for another human being; someone you dislike because they've not been nice to you and whose every action irritates you. It might be someone who you have had to be nice to for a very long time, who keeps getting away with things, knows how to "play the game" and about whom you know that, but for a small amount of digging, someone could find the truth and teach this person a lesson.

'There is a big difference between knowing the truth and telling it. You decide'

Religion

You may not be religious in any way. My religion involves having a good heart and faith in humanity. There are good and bad people in every organisation. Having faith is your faith. Believe in what you believe. If your religion tells you that certain things are right or wrong, then that is fine as long as what you believe does not conflict with the law and the policy of your organisation. If this is the case, revealing wrongdoing becomes easier because of your faith. You may benefit from having someone in your faith that you trust and can turn to for advice, and this can be of great value to you.

17

'Do something amazing. Change someone's life for the better. Expose the truth'

Excitement

There is a particular thrill involved in knowing a secret and then telling it to someone. We have all had conversations where a friend says to you ... "Psst. Do not tell anyone that bla bla bla". You then reply, "I promise, I really promise". Then you meet someone that would like to know what you have to say – you say to them, "Psst. Do not tell anyone. Promise not to tell anyone. I mean promise. Really promise". You then tell all. How do you know that that person is not going to go and tell someone else? You hope they do not. How will you feel if they tell someone in the same way you did? The secret you have may be very difficult to keep. You want to tell everyone and the excitement when you do, mixed with all the other emotions, will be part of this process.

'Trust your heart. Use your head'

Loyalty

Loyalty develops slowly over time. It depends on age, experience, trust, rewards, and family. It has to be based on real actions, not phoney ones.

'Limit their dishonesty because your limit has been reached. Take no more'

Revenge

Revenge is sweet. It involves getting back at someone who has done you a disservice, or someone or something that has upset you. You do not need any other reason to blow the whistle. You just want the person to know they have been found out and there can be no better reason than that. Whatever you do, always tell the truth and no more. Do not embellish the truth to suit your needs as it will come back and bite you. However tempted you may be to tell more than you know, just seeing the wrongdoer caught out or undone by their own actions will be satisfaction enough.

'Systems fail because cheats prosper. Put a stop to it'

Jealousy

Although not a common reason to speak up, it is common enough to feature here. It might be that you work for an organisation where nepotism and the old boy network have got to you over the years. You may have been passed over for promotion, side-lined for political reasons, or there has been a complete disregard for your loyalty and service to the organisation, along with very little recognition of the hard work that you have put in. Could this be your chance to tell the truth and see that person receive some justice? It may well be that you have reached a tipping point on your "axis of anger" and you have seen someone promoted to a point where you think enough is enough.

'Wanted. The truth. Apply yourself'

Money

Some say this is not the main driver. However, this is nonsense. Wave cold, hard cash in front of people and they will talk. Money matters and money talks. Even if someone initially says they do not want money in return for information, in the vast majority of cases, they will take it if offered. To some people it is their main driver, to others it helps them through the month. Some may even give it to charitable cause.

When offered money, the majority of people find it hard to turn down. Information is very difficult to put a price on – how do you value it? This may depend on the amount, the quality, the nature of the situation, and the risk the whistle-blower took to obtain it? Its value is very subjective. To someone who has nothing, any amount may be seen as huge – to a wealthy businessman, it could be seen as insulting. It is a difficult call to make and few people want to be insulted.

In the criminal world, whistle-blowers pay no tax or national insurance. If you had little income and received a large monetary reward, how would you account for this? How could you spend it safely without friends becoming suspicious? How could you store it safely? The management of reward money is a major factor in keeping whistle-blowers safe and rigorous safeguards are put in place to ensure accountability.

On most occasions, whistle-blowers will have their expenses paid, such as the cost of getting to the venue, telephone calls, perhaps a drink or food when meeting their handler. Large amounts of money are generally paid in stages to avoid suspicion from friends and family as to how they obtained such large payments without seemingly working for them. Large amounts must therefore be risk-assessed so that the whistle-blower is not exposed by having to account for them. Small amounts have to be carefully managed so that, for example, drug users do not potentially overdose on the money they have been given. Oh, if money was simple to manage – the root of all evil and good!

The correct use of money is invaluable in terms of gaining outstanding intelligence. You cannot obtain an insight into the activity of those you are interested in by not paying decent amounts of money.

The vast majority of people have a price. What would yours be? £5, £10, £100, or £1000? Would you exchange information in return for money? What information do you have that someone else would pay money for? Could you accept 'blue money'? Would it be a step too far? In my experience very few whistle-blowers refuse money - the majority take it. In any case, who cares? As a covert whistle-blower you do not have to tell anyone.

'Breath in the facts, breath out the truth. Shame the liars'

Is money really the root of all evil? Think of the good a well-placed whistle-blower can do. For example, they could:

- Recover stolen property that is of sentimental value to the owner.

- Arrest someone who has committed a crime.

- Reveal a crime.

- Provide insight into the minds of those who wish to do harm.

How can this be measured? Is it worse to be the informant or the authorities? What you know could be the last, vital piece of information in the intelligence jigsaw. It is all highly subjective, but intrinsically you have to be fair, honest, subject to scrutiny, and full of integrity. The list goes on.

Money is a way of saying thank you. Thank you for your time, thank you for your effort, and thank you for your information. I have never heard someone who manages a whistle-blower say that they have paid too much to someone. If anything, it is normally not enough. The risk people take to pass information on and regularly meet their handler should not be underestimated. The risk of compromise is very real and places whistle-blowers under considerable stress. To be paid small amounts of money on a regular basis - £50, £100 or £150 – is, in my opinion, not worth the gamble. To entrust the authorities with your life is unlikely to be seen as worth the risk. Very few informants I have met have been genuinely satisfied with what they have been given. Everyone always wants more. Authority budgets have been reducing, leading to increased pressure being placed on formal budgets to provide more value for money.

Whistle-blowers will generally never become rich by providing information. The money will help get the car serviced, buy a nice meal, and generally help out with household bills. It is a gesture, no more than that. It is true that some whistle-blowers are given large sums that can make a massive difference, but this is not a common occurrence. Obviously, the more the risk the higher the value of the commodity, and the time saved by the authority is always in favour of the amount paid. The figure is always a round one and never paid until the very last moment. This is for ease of payment and shows that paying for information is not an exact science.

I have known whistle-blowers to be paid considerable amounts that may appear excessive to the public. I can understand the sentiment but, balanced against the time saved trying to catch increasingly sophisticated criminals, I believe this is money well spent. In comparison with not catching people, or even when the authorities are trying to catch people, the rewards paid in relation to the cost to the taxpayer are very small. The press periodically publicise the amount spent on informants, but do not set this against the overall cost of covert policing – a legitimate tactic – and, when used properly, how cost-effective this method of intelligence gathering can be.

'The challenge is doing the right thing. To ignore is doing the wrong thing'

Chapter 4

Other Things That You Might Want To Consider

Will the Organisation Benefit?

Any organisation that values honesty and integrity can only benefit from having policies in place that support members of staff who speak up. Not only does it show that staff have confidence in their management to deal with wrongdoing for the benefit of everyone, they also feel empowered to report wrongdoing. This means that the organisation not only benefits internally by identifying problems with personnel issues and working policies, it also sets an example to other firms in their industry as well as those further afield by showing that their business is ethical and moralistic. It sets a benchmark for dealing with wrongdoing. No-one should be so naïve as to believe that any business with more than one employee will not encounter wrongdoing at some point. It is how the organisation deals with these issues that counts. If it tries to bury them, this can be seen as even worse than having a whistleblowing policy in place to deal with such issues. Everyone knows the truth and intense scrutiny will be placed on those involved in the investigation, which simply increases the pressure.

By speaking up you may be trying to weigh up the personal benefits alongside those for the organisation. Only you can decide where your loyalties lie and what effect you think the wrongdoing you are reporting will have on you and your employer.

'If it doesn't feel or look right it probably isn't'

Therefore, for any organisation that purports to be transparent, honest, and acting with integrity, a robust whistleblowing policy is not just an agenda item that gets pushed to the back of the queue in terms of priority, it is the priority. If it is not, and those working for the organisation do not feel they are able to report wrongdoing, the whole organisation could be taken down. Without such a policy there may well be an increase in absenteeism, staff turnover, grievances that need to be resolved, and a decrease in productivity.

All of these factors (and there are many more) cost time and money. Openness, a willingness to listen, and pro-active engagement with staff means that small issues can be dealt with at an early stage and do not escalate to much larger issues. There will always be some element of disagreement in any team; however, it takes courage from senior members of the organisation to encourage discussion and dialogue at all levels and ensure that, when this occurs, there is meaningful resolution to the issues that have been highlighted.

'The camera never lies but people do.

Expose the truth'

Whistleblowing can occur at all levels of any dispute. It can be overt or covert and have a small or large impact, depending on the disclosure. Employees should be encouraged to speak-up. It should not be seen as a taboo subject, which is simply a policy to cover the backs of management. Whistle-blowers should be pro-actively sought to highlight how an organisation can improve. Whistle-blowers should be seen not as pariahs, but as champions of the cause. They are there to improve the lives of everyone and ensure any wrongdoing is dealt with in a proportionate and fair manner. It is, therefore, sensible to ensure that whistle-blowers are dealt with in a sensitive way, with a framework in place to ensure they remain on course during an investigation. There is a great deal of cynicism about whistleblowing, yet much support for the facts when they emerge. Few want to be known as a grass, but everyone wants to know the gossip. Organisations need to know that this type of gossip reaps benefits for the individual as well as themselves.

'There is another way. The right way'

Into the Unknown

Whenever you enter a conflict, for this is what it may seem like, you should do your research. The more you prepare, the more chance you have of succeeding. Your research into the wrongdoer's strength and weaknesses, their vulnerabilities, and where they may be able to score points (unless you have overwhelming evidence) will give you a considerable advantage. If you fail to do this, you may be opening up yourself up to an immediate defeat. Make sure you have plenty of evidence. You also need to make sure you keep your allies on your side and possibly utilise them as loyal spies as events unfold.

'The sound of your soul will always sing louder than the lies that they tell'

It perhaps seems ironic that you may have felt yourself to have been a spy before this whole episode unfolded - you now need to utilise any spies that can help you. You will find out just how valuable they can be.

Knowing who you are making the disclosure about can take time. You need to consider issues such as how well they are regarded in the organisation, who their allies are, and what sort of reaction you will get if and when they find out it was you who blew the whistle. Are they vindictive? Will they roll over and admit to everything or will they fight tooth and nail to defend their position? Will they try and get back at you another way or will they use one of their allies to do so? Will they make it more difficult for you to detect retaliation? Your enemy may try to use every trick in the book to undermine you.

Whatever happens, one thing is for sure; you will never know until you enter the battle. No battle has ever been entered into without plenty of variables and the unknown being taken into consideration. The future is difficult to predict. You will never know until you try. Furthermore, if the matter of wrongdoing is of such importance, you may not even care what the reaction of the accused will be.

'If you hit the snake it will rear up and try and fight you. It's how you deal with the reaction that determines the outcome'

You may well find that you are stronger than you thought and the battle is not that bad after all. The thought of doing something is normally a lot worse than the actual event. Besides, your evidence may be overwhelming; such as, documentary evidence that cannot be refuted. If that is the case, then what are you worried about?

If your sense of justice and truth is strong and you know you are right, then reveal the truth and see what happens afterwards.

The Script

You know how this goes. You grow up, become qualified, get a job you are pleased about, are possibly a bit nervous about at first, but you soon settle in, make new friends, discover new possibilities, and life seems good. Then things start to unravel a little and what seemed to be a life of eating caviar and drinking champagne suddenly no longer seems so good. The gloss comes off the organisation and you start seeing it in its true colours, warts and all. Then you are caught. You might be on a good salary and have built up loyalty, credibility, and a reputation. You can see a career progression, but you have discovered some unsavoury truth about someone or something.

'There is no illusion. The trick is to say it as it is'

You do not know what to do. Do you do nothing or a little bit of something which you know may help clear your conscience but, in reality, will have little impact? Do you leave the organisation and know that the issue will carry on, or do you do something which will impact massively on you, your family and the organisation? What to do?! You then decide to do something positive and speak up. Then what? What is the script now?

If you have never done this before then you are entering unchartered waters. Where do you find the flow chart that outlines what will happen, how long it all takes and what sanctions could possibly be enforced against those about whom you have made the disclosure? And much of this, like a lot of things in life, is dependent on the personalities involved. How will they react and what will they do?

'There are opinions and there are facts. You cannot change facts. Expose the truth'

In essence, there is no script. You just have to go with the flow and follow your gut instinct. There may be no time frame and, in some cases, no logic that you can follow. To a large extent it really is a case of suck it and see. What will be will be; do not fight the system. Go with it and take from it what you will. Like a lot of challenges in life, you do not know what you will find until you get there. View this episode as another one of life's stories. Unless you are completely immune from feeling, this journey will take place completely outside your comfort zone. Until you go there, you will never know. Help write the script. There is no methodology, no exact science, no well-trodden path you can follow. See the journey as an exploration. There will be no-one to guide you or teach you how to blow the whistle. It is a lonely place that only you will understand. Although I do not know of any support groups, there are books you can read to help you understand where you are and how others have felt.

A Wake-Up Call for Your Conscience

Have you ever thought to yourself- what am I all about? Who am I and what do I represent? What do I believe in? I do not know whether it is an age thing or down to experience, but there comes a point in life where you take stock, reflect, and stand back and look at yourself. Maybe, once you realise who you are, you might start wondering what other people think of you. Although you might like yourself for who you are and what you believe in, you may or may not care what others think of you.

'It takes the few to stand up for the many'

Regardless of what other people think, you portray an image to the world that signifies who you are and what you stand for. Like it or not, others will then judge you based on what you do and say. There are times when you will encounter issues in life that you decide to do something about. I'm not talking about trivial matters; I'm talking about issues that really resonate with you, that reach to the depths of your soul and about which you feel you have to do something. You may not change the course of everything, but you can change your world and make a difference, not only to yourself but to others. Maybe this is the moment where what you have discovered has riled you to the core and you cannot stand it any longer. Not only that, those around you will judge you by your actions. You might not care what they think, but they will judge you all the same.

'When is a lie not a lie? When it's a fact'

Your conscience has come to the fore and you have to decide what to do. To do nothing will be judged possibly as a weakness or siding with the wrongdoer. To sit on the fence is not going to achieve anything other than create ongoing uncertainty. But to do something is a positive step. Some may not like what you do, but do you really care? It's your conscience, your life, and your decision. Be bold and do something. Indecision is frustrating. People may not agree with you, but there are plenty of people in life who cannot make decisions. Ironically, this may be for fear of being criticised.

In a strange way, this journey may be the time that you needed to reflect and find out who you really are. You may already know and this moment simply reaffirms this knowledge. Or perhaps someone gives you a gentle nudge to say, "come on, this is your time". Whatever way you got to this point, now is the time to act. This is no time for procrastination. Just do it.

'Let sleeping dogs lie. Wake them with the truth'

Chapter 5

You Have Decided To Blow The Whistle

Congratulations! You have decided to become a whistle-blower and speak up. You are not the first to report wrongdoing and you will not be the last. Do not feel bad - feel proud. You have joined a growing club, a club whose numbers will only continue to rise. You have decided to make the world a better place. It is a big step but one which will ultimately make you a stronger person.

So what next? Where do you go from here? You will have to think practically about the best way to report wrongdoing within your organisation. Confidential hotlines, speaking to your line manager, or contacting your union are just a few of the options that may be available to you.

One thing is for certain – there will be many people giving advice about the best way for you to get through this. Many will be well intentioned; however, the strongest piece of advice I can give you is this – whatever information you have in your head, write it down straight away. This will be beneficial to you both as evidence and in a therapeutic way - in much the same way writing this book was for me. I have outlined below some practical tasks that can help you through your journey:

- Write down what you know. To see it all written down is both gratifying and makes more sense. Words will otherwise just whizz round your head, around and around with no outlet. To help you do this, be sure to keep any evidential documentation safe.

- There are many quotes available online to help keep you sane and reassure you that you are not alone. Twitter is great in this respect with numerous feeds offering some fantastically inspiring quotes.

- Consider using welfare and counselling services in your community or online. Doctors, private counsellors, and occupational health departments in larger organisations can all be sources of help.

- Mindfulness exercises on You Tube.

- Take regular exercise.

- Talk regularly to someone you trust.

'Sometimes you have to travel the most difficult route to reach the better destination'

Be Well Prepared

For any journey you have to prepare. The timing, the method, the research, the places - these are all vitally important factors in ensuring that the result is what you want or at least can best envisage. The journey that a whistle-blower embarks on is no different in this regard. Make sure you know what the process entails. Ask yourself practical questions such as:

- How do I blow the whistle?
- To whom do I blow the whistle?
- What happens when I do?
- How will I feel?
- What will happen to my friends?
- Will I need counselling?
- Should I take medication?

There are many factors on the journey that are hard to comprehend beforehand as you might not have had the time or forethought to adequately prepare. Like any journey, there will also be unexpected twists and turns and things that you cannot prepare for. There may be a massive change of heart by the perpetrators that means your issue is resolved before any action is taken, or there could be politics involved; when you blow the whistle others may be unaware of your position in the organisation and what the implications will be when you make a disclosure. Whatever happens and however well you plan, you must keep your wits about you

One thing is certain - no two whistleblowing scenarios are the same. This is due to differences in people, organisational structure and the nature of the information you are providing. You can read books, seek information from the internet, read organisational policy and speak to friends, but the acid test ultimately entails going through the process. And it is just a process. Organisations have procedures in place that deal with everyday events. Unless they are fundamentally corrupt, the chances are that whoever deals with your disclosure is likely to be checking it on a daily basis. Work with them, not against them simply to be bloody minded. You need them to be on your side. Part of your preparation involves find out who will be dealing with your disclosure. It always helps to know their history and experience and could mark the difference between an investigation being poorly or well managed.

'Do not be sorry for their mistakes. Apologise for nothing. Reveal the truth'

Batten Down the Hatches

What can you do to prepare? Have you got coping strategies in place? Do you have a checklist? What follows is not an exhaustive list but may help you to cope:

- Books
- Routine – mind and body
- Diary
- Medication
- Evidence
- Support network
- An exit strategy
- Contact details for local organisations
- A thick skin!

Have No Regrets

When you start the whistleblowing journey you will be full of doubt, full of anger, and want to see justice done. You want to tell someone what has happened or is still happening. You may not even care what the consequences are for yourself. You spill the beans, sit back, and watch things unfold. Then the enormity and reality of what you have done begins to sink in. You have hit the metaphorical nuclear button and people start running for cover. They cannot believe what you have done, others deny all knowledge, and some turn against you. Only yesterday the status quo was one of normality and everyday routines were taking place as usual. If you had not done what you had done life would have been so much easier.

Then you might start wondering why you have done this. What would it have been like if you had not pressed the button: perhaps things might have improved on their own? If this happens – STOP. Take yourself back to the time when things were terrible, when you couldn't bear to see injustice and remember that things would have been much worse if you had not done something about it.

Never regret doing what you have done. It will make things much, much worse for you. It will mean that those you have reported on will make your life even worse. You will lose sleep, perhaps some friends, and the wrongdoers will be winning. Remain steadfast in your resolve. Fight the good fight and keep your sanity. You can never go back and change things. If you regret what you have done, the person or people that you set out to help will not thank you if they think you are putting your own interests before theirs.

39

Life would be so much easier if people looked the other way and let those who commit wrongdoing get away with it. It may be that, if they are doing what you have uncovered, this is part of a general charade they have created in other aspects of their life.

You may even hear on the grapevine that those you have reported are saying that they are not affected by what you have done. Do not believe this. Although they might not say it publicly, they will be thinking it privately. Everyone knows the truth, even the perpetrators, but they are the ones struggling to bury it. You are the brave person that has exposed them. Have no regrets about doing so.

'Be remembered for the right reason. That you were the brave one'

Keep Your Word

There is nothing worse than someone saying they are going to do something and then not doing it. People moan about issues, other people, even the weather. However, there are some things people moan about that they can do something about. There is no point moaning if you do not do anything. This includes your personal life, your income, your health, and so on. It also includes wrongdoing. If you continually witness something that is plainly wrong and it continues and you still carry on moaning, there must surely come a point where you cannot even bear the sound of your own voice. Trust me, if it gets to that point, others will have realised long before you have. So what should you do? Either say nothing and maintain the status quo or speak up. Saying nothing is not a real option, especially if there is a criminal element to wrongdoing or bullying in the workplace. There is only one real choice and it is staring you in the face.

If you have confided in others that this is what you are going to do, then do it! For if you do not, there is no need to even bother mentioning the subject again. Remember when you were at school and a teacher threatened you with detention if you did not do your homework? If you then failed to do your homework and no detention followed, there was no deterrent. Nor was there any future deterrent. Well, this situation is no different. Your friends and colleagues will always remember your threat to report wrongdoing: they may have encouraged you to do it and you may have said you would do it. Therefore, if you change your mind, how would that look? You know the answer. As a leader, a motivator, and an example to others, you will look weak and your authority will be undermined. Furthermore, if you are a leader you have responsibility and you are being paid more as a result of this. There is therefore no option other than to do the right thing. The situation may have got so bad at work that you have become boxed in and have no other option. Come out fighting and show yourself, your team, and your organisation what you are really made of.

Keep a Positive Outlook

It is not only vitally important to have a positive outlook in life; it is even more important to try and carry this through when you have reported misconduct. Mindfulness is a great way of keeping everything in perspective. Remember that the whistleblowing journey is just one aspect of your life, however overwhelming it may seem at that time. You have to be able to keep a sense of perspective. It may seem to you like it will never end, that it is the most important thing ever to have happened to mankind, and that it is all consuming. That may well be the case for you, but take a step away from your life, adopt a helicopter view, a different way of seeing things and you will realise that, in the great scheme of things, life goes on. Remind yourself that, in terms of the history of humanity, the issue that you are reporting on will probably not alter the course of the planet. This is not to devalue what you are doing, for it is important that righteous people like you stand up for what is good and proper. However, in reality the likelihood is that the rest of the planet will never get to hear of the good that you have done.

However, a positive outlook is not achieved by telling yourself that no-one outside your world cares about what you are doing. It is far more fundamental and involves friends and family, maintaining a healthy diet, perhaps watching your favourite comedy on a box set, turning off the news before bed so that you do not go to sleep thinking about negative things, listening to upbeat music, doing a good deed for others, planning your next holiday, or maybe even planning a holiday for those that have helped you through this journey as a thank you.

Do not forget that, although it may be difficult for you, it will also be difficult for those close to you who do not want to see you go through the anguish that you are experiencing. To treat them when everything has ended is a way of recognising their support, as it is highly likely that you will have confided in them to a degree and this will have had an effect on them too. Stay humble, generous, and compassionate to those around you for without them this process would have been a whole lot worse.

Act Like You Mean Business

There is nothing more a wrongdoer wants than someone reporting what they have done in a half-hearted manner. Any sign of weakness is an opportunity they will relish. Take the example of a hungry lion waiting to prey on the weakest member of the herd so that he can show how strong he is. Do not let that be you. Stand tall, stand proud, and let them know that you are here for the long haul. No-one is going to push you around, for that is exactly what they are hoping for. They hope you will back down and quietly go and sulk in the corner. They also hope that you will apologise and say it has all been a terrible mistake and misunderstanding. That is exactly what you are not going to do.

'The truth costs nothing but gives a lot. Play your part'

You know what you have in terms of evidence, witnesses and the strength of your self-belief. You know that if anything comes back at you once you have poked the hornet's nest, you can rebuff any accusations that come your way because you know what things are like. They have lied to get to this point and they will lie to try and discredit you. Who do they think they are? Why should they get away with it? You also suspect they will try every trick in the book to do this.

You know that they will attempt to deny everything and one of the tactics they employ will be to try to discredit you. It is therefore imperative that you give it 100%. No ifs, buts or maybes. You know you are right so will stick to your guns. This means portraying a professional, positive, competent, and passionate image with no weaknesses, otherwise those around you will be less inclined to support you. That is human nature.

There may be some who will support you whatever the circumstances; however, you need the support of as many people as possible, including those on the periphery of the situation. They are the ones who may be wavering in their support for you and, as such, are important. Any successful person or leader will have confidence in their beliefs and you cannot afford to be any different in this regard. Set your stall out, be strong and act like you mean business.

Have Faith in Yourself

Self-belief is vital if you are to remain resolute in the process you are undertaking. If you do not believe in yourself then who is going to believe in you? At the beginning of the journey you will be so enraged, so motivated to tell the truth, and so fired up that you will not even envisage the end goal. You might not even care! The release you will have is what you will be seeking in the short term. But there will be times when you question yourself and your decision to reveal all. Not only that, you may question your sanity and others may do so as well! Why have you put yourself through this, as well as your family and friends? Your time will be consumed thinking about the subject before, during, and after the process. You may be wondering whether it is all worth it.

Surely the easy thing to do would be to walk away, turn a

blind eye, and just ignore the issue. However, inside you know you have done the right thing. Keep faith in yourself and remind yourself that once you have pressed the button there is no going back. As part of your routine you might want to have a daily motivational quote handy that you can relate to or you may occasionally re-read the disclosure you made to someone about the wrongdoing. This will help reaffirm that what you have done was correct and will help bring back the feelings of injustice and the intolerance that you or others have experienced.

Regularly chat with your friends and family about what you are feeling and reaffirm that what you have done is the right thing. They will tell you the truth and help you through the journey. Keep the faith.

'What starts as a trickle becomes a river of truth and by that time you cannot stop the flow'

The Importance of Self-Worth

Without you there would be no reporting. There would be no witness to the wrongdoing and there would be no possible further revelations. There would also be no further support to those that might follow you and there would be no future after your revelation. Wrongdoers do not want to get caught. They want to cover up and practice their deceit. They do it for self-gain and do not worry about others who might be affected. They see themselves as more important than you; that their wrongdoing is irrelevant to your wellbeing.

It is therefore important that you take care of yourself and realise just how important you are to you and those around you. Look after yourself in both mind and body. Set time aside for yourself. This may seem alien as you have just reported on someone who has looked after themselves. You might worry what others will think of you if you do something for yourself. However, what happens if you do not? Flip the situation over and think about the alternative outcome. I'm not saying change your personality to become selfish and self-centred, just realise the value of taking time out for yourself. If you do not, your friends and family may think that, although you are generous with your time for others, you are a bit of a mug. They may think that the reason the wrongdoer did what they did was because they saw you as a soft touch, that you wouldn't report them for what they were doing, and that they could continue to get away with it.

You have to be you and you have to remain steadfast. If you do not look after yourself that steadfastness may start to wane and you will feel bad and even apologetic for what you have done. That is a bad position from which to recover. If you have never had self-worth, it can be difficult to achieve. If you have had it and are trying to regain it, that too can be a struggle. Furthermore, if you are somewhere in between, that can be even harder because you do not know whether to go up or down!

Regardless of how you measure self-worth, you will know how you look after yourself and whether you are spending as much time on yourself as you can. Even if you are, are you doing the right things to make you feel better? If so – great. If not, try something different until you do. It will be worth it in the end!

Enjoy the Ride

Consider what happens when you go to the theme park. You pay for a ticket, go in, look around, see what there is to see, and then decide to go on a ride. Depending on your attitude you may pick something you feel safe with, something that you have gone on before, or maybe someone with you dares you to have a go on a novel ride. Perhaps you are a thrill seeker and cannot wait to get on the scariest ride in the park. You can see where this is going!

Being a whistle-blower can be the same as buying a ticket for the scariest ride in the park. You probably haven't been on it before, but you know it will probably be scary. You also know that you will be protected and safe. As long as you strap in, listen to the safety briefing, follow the instructions and sit tight, you will be absolutely fine. The scariest ride is not for the faint hearted, nor is it one you can get off once it has started. However, you know it will come to an end at some point, and you also know there are safety measures in place to look after you. You also know that it is your choice to get on. Although you may have been persuaded to some degree, ultimately it is always your choice. You will also find things out about yourself that you did not know. Qualities such as strength, resilience, persistence, a deep sense of justice and tenacity to name but a few.

I would not recommend whistleblowing as a way of discovering qualities you did not know you had. I am sure that there are easier ways of discovering these qualities, although the ride will, in time, allow you to reflect upon and realise the person that you really are. In adversity, the real you will come to the fore and you will discover who you really are. Others will see it in you as well. Be proud of who you are. Do not be scared to find the real you. Believe that only good can come out of this process. Look positively on this, see it as an experience about which only you know how you have done – not the outcome of your disclosure, but how you have coped with the ride. Did you want to get off but could not, did you want it to go on longer because you enjoyed it? Did it take you outside your comfort zone and enable you to see life through a different set of eyes? You bought the ticket, now get on the ride – it is your choice.

'They hide the facts; you seek the truth'

Closing Ranks

There will be an inevitable defence made against any claim you make. Even if the wrongdoing is so obvious someone would have to be stupid to deny the charges, there will be some excuse made as to why it was done. Furthermore, as in any closed group, people will come to the defence of a colleague who they see is in trouble because they have worked together over a period of time and may have got to know them socially. They will probably not know the real truth. Thus, it is inevitable that the closing ranks scenario will arise.

When this happens be prepared. Ranks and management have a habit of doing this. How many times in history have you seen a complete denial of the obvious for it then to be laid out with irrefutable evidence? What you rarely see from people who did not question the facts and then get told the truth is a subsequent apology. And why would they? They may say that they could not have known. They may claim that they were hoodwinked by the wrongdoer or even turned a blind eye to the wrongdoing so as not to upset the apple cart?

'Some said and didn't. Be the one who says and does. Expose the truth'

Conspiracy theories will abound regarding what really happened but that is not something you need to worry about. All you need to be concerned with is your health and well-being, not the gossip about which you can do nothing. What will make the outcome sweeter for you is when you show that, for all the checks and balances an organisation has in place to try and deflect wrongdoing, you are the one that has unlocked the secret. For every process that involves a human being, there is another human being who will find a way around that process. There is nothing better than a well-placed person like yourself to provide the details someone else thinks they can hide. History tells us that this has always been the case and so it will prove in the future.

George Orwell's 'Animal Farm' (1945) brilliantly illustrates how power can corrupt. People do not think that they will be found out - but they are. The issue of closing ranks does not help matters and often you will find that there is a real loyalty between managers. In any case, once the truth emerges people will start to distance themselves from the wrongdoer.

'Fake news. You choose'

Paranoia

One of the first things you may experience once you have filed your report is the paranoia of revenge from those you have reported on or their associates. What will they do, what will they say, who is saying what, and will they come after you? This could be at your place of work or at home. It could even get to the point where you may think that you are under surveillance, that your phone calls are being listened to, that your allies are being told not to talk to you because you may be trying to influence them as potential witnesses, and that the organisation may try every trick in the book to try and discredit you. Let me assure you this – it is all highly unlikely to be true.

It is even possible that, as a reaction, you may be subject to a police raid based on some spurious piece of information just to intimidate you and get you to withdraw your allegation. All of this may seem worse at night (things generally are). However, if you have nothing to hide, are squeaky clean and there is no dirt to dish on you, all these thoughts will just be in your head. This is the 21st century and ethically sound organisations would not want to be involved in these practices. This is not to say that these practices do not take place, therefore it is only right to prepare and remain on your guard.

In my experience, any paranoia you have will exist only in your head. It is important that you keep things in perspective and believe that the whole world is not against you. The resources and cost to an organisation to try and discredit what you have disclosed would be completely disproportionate in relation to what you have said and the ramifications for the organisation would be immense. The bad PR that it would generate would not be in any organisation's interest, e.g., possibly employing private detectives, forensic investigators, and so on.

One of the worst things you might experience is waiting for a reply to an email you sent asking about the progress of any enquiry. This may seem to take forever and the wait can be unbearable. Remember, however, that the world is carrying on regardless of what you have disclosed. Be patient. Whistle-blower disclosures take time to investigate and the course of justice can be painfully slow. Keep strong, keep the faith, and believe me when I say they are not after you. Remember that you are the one that has made the disclosure, not the other way around!

'Push the button. Expose the truth'

Chapter 6

Practical Tips

Respect Your Colleagues

You may not really know them, or even like them, but everyone has a story to tell. Work brings together people from different backgrounds with a different history. This makes them the people they are, but the one thing that unites them and you is the respect they need to show for each other. This makes the team function. It creates harmony, unity, and a productive environment. The greatest respect you can have for a colleague is to help them by supporting them. This might be unpalatable if there is history between you but if you can help them in some way to have a better time at work, in most cases their better work life will transfer to their home life. Speaking up could be one of your greatest achievements. There may be no greater intangible reward then respect from your colleagues for doing the right thing - you will get this both for reporting wrongdoing and for being seen as the one who has actually stood up and been counted. Be the person that others would want to fight alongside in the trenches.

'It is better to confront the truth than avoid it'

Motivation and Influence

There may be people you know who will support you through your journey. There may be others that you think may support you and do not, and there may be those who you know will not. Whoever and wherever they are, it is important that you take as many as possible with you on your journey. For it may be the case that, when you take the lid off the wrongdoing, offers of support will be forthcoming. You may find that people have had the same or similar experiences and, were it not for you being the first to step forward, they would not have had the courage to speak out.

So how do you go about motivating and influencing these people? What can you do to help them through their journey as well as yours? My advice is this:

1. Be yourself. Be the person that people know you are - sincere, honest, hardworking, and supportive. If you believe in yourself others will be more inclined to do the same.

2. Remain humble. It is not you taking on the world but you uncovering dishonesty and integrity that is the issue. Do not go around showing everyone how good you are for what you are doing. You are standing up for everyone. It is the principle behind what has happened that is important - your role was to highlight the issue. If you start telling others what

they should be thinking or saying you may alienate people. People do not necessarily want to be told what to do but they may react well to good advice. It is, after all, a massive step to take to speak up and you will probably be further down the path of self-justification than they are. It is a fine balance to maintain. For example, if the issue is bullying and they have been subject to it, the last thing they want is to feel under more pressure as a result of being told to expose the truth.

3. Keep in regular contact with those that support you. What initially may be massive news will soon become old news and, if you are absent from work because of what you have done, you do not want to forget these people; otherwise they may feel they are being abandoned. The process of influence extends right through the journey from start to finish.

Building Relationships

I never really understood the power and importance of networking until I blew the whistle. You can read about networking and experience it in an unconscious way; however, there will be times in your life when it suddenly becomes apparent that all the people you have met, both inside and outside of work, mean a lot more to you that you might have realised. The snippets of time or conversations that you have had over days, weeks, months, or years suddenly become more important and the reason for this is that your life has been brought sharply into focus. More than ever, you will need people around you to support you, advise you and reassure you.

You are out of necessity building a network from which to fight back at the wrongdoers. A network of people that you can trust and turn to and ask, "am I doing the right thing or have I overstepped the mark and am going mad?" From friends at work to people you have not seen for ages, the reaction you will receive may be as wide and diverse as you can imagine. Yet all are people that you trust to give sound advice.

'The truth is strength. Do not be scared to be strong'

Do not be scared to listen to the "critical friend". You know, those friends that will sometimes tell you the painful truth. People within your network will often not even know each other, but the common bond will be you. You are the one person they all have in common, someone they respect and like and will help out. So do not be scared to ask for the odd favour, for their time and advice. It is all too easy to retreat into a shell and not ask for help. After all, isn't this what friends are for? Life is full of ups and downs – friends will get you through the hard times and they will get you through this.

Networks take time to build and I do not mean in just a cynical way. You have built up a network primarily to get you through difficult times such as this! You share laughs, possibly a common interest and socialise together: this is just part of that process. Do not be backwards in coming forwards. It might seem like the whole world is against you sometimes, but it certainly isn't. You will discover new friends along this journey as well as building on the relationships you have had for years. See this as an opportunity to extend your network even further to ensure you develop as a person. As hard as it may seem, this can be treated as an opportunity to progress in life.

Be Loyal

You will be of a certain age, with certain experiences and life skills. Unless you are a hermit, you will not have achieved your goals in life without the help of others. As a person you are a mixture of yourself and a sprinkling of others who have influenced you in life. All these factors make you the person that you are.

And now you have decided to speak up. Your friends and family have put up with your moaning, coming home late from work, having sleepless nights, and maybe being absent from work due to stress. The last thing they need from you is any form of disloyalty. You need all the help you can get and you need these people to support your disclosure, from possible moral support through to enhanced physical support such as providing evidence. The journey is not an easy one so keep in touch with friends. Make sure you do not do anything stupid and make sure you reward others for being there for you. This could be anything from buying them a coffee when you are out to a weekend away with your partner. Be loyal to their emotions as well and do not forget to ask them how they are.

'Make yourself heard above the din of deceit. Let the truth prevail'

Believe it or not, this time is not just about you. There are other lives going on around you, with all the stresses and strains that entails. Be loyal to your relationships for they will be a great strength to you, not only now but in the future when the whistleblowing case is over. Loyalty works both ways and takes a long time to build. It can quite easily be undone if you do not keep your eye on the ball. In any stressful situation you see the worst and best in people. Let others see the best in you. You want to be remembered for who you are, not what you said you could be.

Do not let yourself down by becoming too miserable about your own situation. I know this can be a difficult thing to remember when you are caught in the middle of the battle but remember that you have all the right attributes - do not start creating bad ones. If you are loyal to others, they will be loyal to you and you will reap the rewards. Loyalty cannot be measured in centimetres or inches. It cannot be seen, but it can be felt. It is an intangible that you need to keep. Do not underestimate its value.

Find Some Music

One of the most inspirational things you can do to keep your sanity is to listen to music. This can be uplifting and can make us sing and dance. It can take you from a dark place to one which is full of light. It has the power to please you, make you believe, and invoke memories. The lyrics do not have to be relevant to where you are or how you feel at that time. It can be a certain guitar riff or a great piece that takes you to a better place. It could be a song from your childhood that makes you happy or a track that takes you back to an amazing holiday.

It may seem like a strange thing to do, but it really does work. Try going for a road trip to give you the space to try an album without any distractions. Turn off your mobile phone and enjoy the music. How often do you have an excuse to do something that makes you feel better? A bit of 'you' time. Music can take you away and is something in which you can absorb yourself. Find a random track or download one you have just heard on the radio. Although this might sound a bit strange – you could even try to write a lyric that reflects how you feel. Try reading the lyrics of songs you like and really think about them. How about making a play-list of all the uplifting and inspiring songs that you know? One of these might just be the thing that strikes the right chord at that time.

However, what inspires you at one particular time might not do so in another. It might just be that the songs you choose now you will look back on later and see as a turning point in a period that, as difficult as it may be now, will be seen as one that was a force for good. If one particular track stands out, that could be the one that works for you. Start playing and enjoy!

Routine

Keeping your sanity during a prolonged period spent witnessing wrongdoing then deciding what to do about it, reporting it and worrying while you wait for something to happen, is important to your wellbeing. At some point you may think you are going mad or insane.

Uncovering and then reporting wrongdoing destabilises your life. It is a very brave thing to do to stand up and be counted and is very much out of the ordinary. Establishing a routine in your life helps keep the everyday "normal" and differentiates the whistleblowing as "abnormal". It is important not to blur the two, however difficult that may be.

'Where there is truth there is hope. Play your part'

It may be as simple as making sure that your bedtime routine is the same every night. Lack of sleep will make the day harder to get through, so it might be useful to try some medication, either from your pharmacy or a natural remedy. Night times are always the worst time as this is when you mull things over and over. When the day breaks and you have other distractions, the world appears to be a better place.

As well as coping strategies such as a night-time routine you may also find it useful to read motivational quotes or to practice mindfulness or yoga. You may well find that incorporating these strategies into a daily or weekly routine helps you cope with the pressure. Physical activity helps with anxiety. If you do not already have an exercise regime, this may be a good time to start. This is not to say go for broke and become a fitness freak; even a gentle stroll around where you live or along a familiar route will give you some headspace in which to gather your thoughts, put life in perspective, and keep things "normal". Having a routine will allow you time for yourself, help keep you in control of certain episodes of your life and enable you to do the things that you want.

You may even want to do the things you have always been meaning to do. Once a week, make a point of visiting somewhere new – a nature reserve or a place of interest that is on your to-do list that you have always put off visiting. The routine you establish becomes your reward for reporting wrongdoing. You see a benefit in reporting someone else's behaviour and, as such, you do something for yourself. Out of a negative comes a positive.

Keep a Diary

Before you know it, you have blown the whistle and the investigation has come to a close. An outcome has been arrived at, but whether justice has been served remains to be seen. However, what has happened in the meantime - where has the stress gone? All the hours and days that have passed have become a distant memory, so it is important to keep a diary. As laborious as it may be, this will enable you to keep track of everything that has happened on your journey. It will enable you to store your thoughts and will enable you to reflect on your journey. There may be occasions during this process that you might need to provide evidence of retaliation by your organisation that contravenes legislation relating to 'Protected Disclosure'.

You might find keeping a diary to be a form of therapy, a way of helping to clear your head of the thoughts you have. It may also be a way of providing a legacy to others who may follow in your footsteps. When the process is over, it may also help encourage people who find themselves in a similar position and enable organisations to develop best practice to ensure the highest of standards. For instance, policies may be improved so that whistleblowing is encouraged within an organisation. A diary will also act as a debrief memoir for when your emotions are particularly raw and when you feel most aggrieved, perhaps even scared about what the future may hold in terms of repercussions at work and how your health is being affected, e.g., records of doctor's appointments.

Time flies and before you know it all the detail you thought you could never forget will become blurred and you will probably only remember the salient points. Keep a diary in whatever form you think best but, whatever you do, keep it relevant and real. Make sure you have it to hand for easy access. You will find it cathartic, as I have, and it will ensure you sustain good mental health. See it as a metaphorical squidgy stress ball!

'Keep going for those who couldn't for one day they will thank you'

Gather Your Evidence

This sounds a bit obvious, but when you make your disclosure who is going to believe you? Anyone can make things up. There may be all sorts of rumours floating around. What you need is some sort of evidence, some way of proving the facts. You do not need to be a detective or a super sleuth – you just need something that will be meaningful to another person. This is the case both before and possibly after your disclosure. Before is self-explanatory – this includes documentation, emails, photographs, diary entries, witness names, and so on. However, you may also find things out post-disclosure; things that you had not even previously thought of that may now be relevant – things that you had forgotten or new pieces of evidence that you did not know existed. New witnesses may be forthcoming who may hold vital testimony to events you had heard about but which only they were privy to. There may be audio recordings of conversations others may have made that you were unaware of. How satisfying it is when you realise that, at a time when you thought you were acting and observing in isolation, all along there were others who were also collecting evidence.

It is important that you keep all your evidence safe. Imagine if you were to inadvertently leave it lying around only for it to fall into the wrong hands. Make sure that you keep it under lock and key. However, a word of caution. Make sure that you fully understand your organisational policy with regard to accessing data that you may use as evidence. There is no point gathering your evidence only to find that you could be held accountable for breaking organisational policy. You have to make sure you are squeaky clean and that there are no skeletons in your closet. You do not want anything coming back on you that could stick. In my case, the accused tried this but failed spectacularly when I produced evidence refuting their claim. This was an example of using what I had not even considered as evidence beforehand to good effect. Evidence is a crucial part of your armoury. It is the main weapon you have against the wrongdoers. All the angst that is part of the journey will be worthless if nothing is proved. You have to help the investigation as much as the investigators have to help you.

Find A New Hobby

Out of the bad always comes some good. It is a question of mindset. You could wallow in self-pity and go around criticising everything about your life, work, family, and so on. But what is this going to achieve? It will just make you feel worse: not only you but the people around you as well. So whether you remain at work or you are off work with symptoms related to whistleblowing, find something pleasant to distract you. A new hobby is a good place to start.

Do something for yourself. You may have been so absorbed with the wrongdoing for such a long period of time that you have not been able to think about anything else. This is the chance for you to take back control of your life and your enjoyment of it – it is a chance for you to put two fingers up to the wrongdoers and say, "thank you very much for this opportunity". However the wrongdoing has manifested itself, if it was not for their arrogance, you would not now be enjoying yourself more than ever before! It can be a hard concept to try and understand and is even more difficult to implement, but it is well worth the effort.

You may choose to take up a hobby such as improving your fitness, writing, cooking, or photography or even taking that opportunity to travel to a place you have always meant to go to but have never had the time. Use this as the opportunity and excuse to do it, and do not be shy to tell people why you are doing it. They will be happy for you because they want you to be happy. To coin a well-known phrase- "don't let the bastards grind you down!"

There are many doomsters in life that will take any chance they can to see you suffer. Show them another side of you - that this episode will not break you – in fact it will make you stronger. Show the world that you are happy. It will make people believe in you even more and that you are not worried about anything, despite how tough this can be at times. Show them that you are settled into your new hobby and are enjoying it. Take a look back every so often and thank your lucky stars that you are personally better for this experience (no matter how hard this may be at first!)

'Reveal not conceal for there lies the truth'

The Depths of Despair

Although you have decided that enough is enough and you have to tell someone what is going on, you may not be prepared for how things progress. Taking that leap of faith by reporting wrongdoing and hoping that someone or somebody will take what you have said seriously is a massive step.

Whether you are a glass half-full or glass half-empty person, you may have never felt so helpless. One moment you are in control of a career as well as your hopes and emotions, next you are entering into a place you have never been before: a journey into the unknown. How will you feel, how will you react, and will you ever come out the other side?

There may be times when you think, "what have I done?" Was this process all worth it? I went from a normal life and career to one that was turned upside down by what I had done. You may feel a huge amount of anxiety, paranoia, fatigue, tiredness and, above all, a feeling of why me?! You may wonder why your life has come to this! How did you get to this point? They never told you about this as an option in the career's library at school!

But you will come out the other side a better person, a stronger person. You may never have felt so low, so lonely, or so isolated, but try to think of it as part of life's rich tapestry. The experience will make you more resilient, more ready to amaze yourself and others, and you will come out of the process with your credibility as a good person, a principled person and a decent human being enhanced. Not that you wanted this to be the aim, but you know that whatever the outcome, you have done the right thing. You may have thoughts you never imagined you could have and feel that you have lost your sanity. It is important to tell you that it happened to me and I came out the other side. Stay strong, stay humble, stay determined, and stay resolute. They will not win. The only winner is you. For the truth will prevail – it is just that getting to that point can be difficult.

Witnesses

These are an amazing asset. Look after your witnesses but do not leave yourself open to accusations of bias or coaching. They can in turn support you, look after you, and make sure that you are not going mad. Without their support you will find the journey so much harder. They can be your rock, your lifeline to reality and, if you are absent from work, a way to keep in touch with what is going on. They can provide further evidence if required and serve as a source of inspiration. They are a shoulder to cry on, a sounding board, and can be straight-talking. They can be a confidante and an ally when the storm breaks.

Make sure you treat them with dignity and respect, something that may have been lacking in any wrongdoer they are providing testimony against. You may also find witnesses in the most unexpected of places. People you may never have even thought of suddenly appear on the radar. People that owe you a favour, who you used to work with, and who see you as a decent person. There may also be people to whom you gave an opportunity to become witnesses, but for unknown reasons they decided not to assist. This may be because of intimidation, further bullying, promotion, career implications, or litigation they are already involved with against the organisation. As such, and although you may be disappointed with their reasons, you have to respect their decision. You cannot persuade or cajole. Remember to remain independent from the investigation. You also may feel it is important to disclose not only specific facts when issues occurred but also how people were made to feel; for example, if bullying was going on. It is easy to forget in the heat of the moment when you become frustrated with wrongdoing just how the little things you feel are incidental are massive issues to someone else.

By pointing these things out, colleagues will feel that maybe they are not so isolated after all and you have a bond, an understanding of each other's issues. Try not to get frustrated when witnesses that you have named, and even those that you have not, are not spoken to for days, weeks, or even months after you have made your disclosure. Frustrating as it may be, investigations take time to gather pace. You have to put yourself in the shoes of the investigators and wait for procedures to be followed. Witnesses can be a great source of strength: you are not alone. There are others out there who also know the truth.

Chapter 7

Conclusion

Would You Do It Again?

You might think this is the end of the journey. Never say never. Is this a journey you never want to go on again? Well, maybe. Very few people would ever set out to find something to blow the whistle on. Not if you knew what it would entail!

But ask yourself this question. If I came across wrongdoing again, what would I do? Would you ignore it and look away because of what you have just been through? Think about it. It might just be that little bit easier the second time around. Maybe you wouldn't come across it because your reputation for reporting wrongdoing means those committing it might purposely avoid you. Or would you do it again for the sake of justice? It is your call. Your attitudes and values towards others may have been reinforced during this process. Perhaps that is attributable to age, experience, or a bit of both. The journey may have inspired a degree of creativity in you that you did not think you possessed. Hopefully, it has not made you a more cynical person.

See the process as an investment in your future. A chance to make new contacts, to break free from the norm. A chance also to plan for your future, to possibly re-brand yourself and a realisation that your work ethic, which may have been waning prior to this journey as a result of what you have witnessed, has become that much stronger.

'When the dust has settled, they know what they did and you know what you did'

Reflect

This is a good point at in which to reflect on this period in your life. Your mind is thinking straight once again. The world has returned to normal. So what have you learnt? What have you learnt about yourself and about others? What have you gained from this and what have you possibly lost? If you write down a list of all the positives and negatives it might look something like this:

Positives	Negatives
Realised how strong I am.	That it temporarily affected my health.
Realised how resilient I am.	Might have affected your career.
Realised how motivated I am.	May have been investigated.
Realised how passionate I am.	May have had your privacy affected.
Realised how much I appreciate my friends.	May have had your life laid bare.

Realised how I value my health.	May have been shunned.
Realised how much I care about my environment.	May have been accused and been subject to revenge.
Realised how much I care about others.	Stress.
Realised how much I believe in right and wrong.	Uncertainty.
Realised how much I value the basic things in life.	May feel low and isolated.
Realised how much I need to work.	
Realised how much I value the trust I put in others.	
Realised how much my family mean to me.	
Gave me a new purpose.	
Gave me a new hobby.	
Made new friends.	

The list goes on. You can see how the positives far outweigh the negatives. So it's a winner! The wrongdoing stops and you gain so much. Who would have thought at the beginning of the journey that this could happen? Why, therefore, are there not more people blowing the whistle? The answer is easy - because it is one of the hardest things you can do.

Back to Normality

Your life returns to some sort of normality. If you have been absent from work, you will now go back. Life returns to how it was before and the dust has settled. You will be surprised. There will be colleagues who you sort of know at work, maybe a little outside work, who engage you in conversation. They may ask you what happened and how you feel. You explain what happened and how you feel and they say you did the right thing. They say that you were brave, that something needed to be done and that whatever you reported could not have continued. They may also say that the perpetrators should not have got away with it for so long. This is all well and good, but where were they if they had also known what was happening? Whatever you do, do not judge them because of their lack of action. Everyone has to do this in their own time and will do it in relation to their own circumstances. It is not for you to judge. Remain humble and present a balanced viewpoint. Be understanding. It is not about revenge or winning – it is about telling the truth. Whistleblowing was the next logical step in whatever position you found yourself in.

What Happens When You Return to Work?

The day comes when you either have to return to work or you start a new job. How will you feel, what will your thoughts be, and how will you cope? Do you feel strong enough to return to work and have you been deemed medically fit to do so? If you have, you may want to consider the following:

- Will you see the wrongdoer and if so, how will you feel?
- Will you be able to perform your role?
- How will you cope with work colleagues who have

been affected by the wrongdoing?

- Will you be oversensitive to anything you may feel is a reactive response?

- Will your colleagues mistrust you regarding any slight misdemeanour? They may do out of a fear you may report them.

- How long will it be before you think life will return to normal?

These are just a few of the factors you may wish to consider before you return to work. It may also help to write down your thoughts, for this will not be easy. This journey has probably been one of the most difficult periods of your life – the uncertainty, the prolonged agony of the outcome. All these factors will have taken their toll.

On the flip side, reflect on the positives – what you have learnt about yourself and others, what new skills you might have learnt, and what a positive future you may now have. Reflect on the respect people now have for you for standing up for justice and equality and not letting the wrongdoers carry on, despite risking the security of working for your organisation. You have grown as a person.

In my case a new future emerged from the process and a new way of looking at life. You may have learnt who you truly are; that you are principled enough to stand up and be counted and that you respect others too. If you are in a position of responsibility at work, ignoring wrongdoing means you are as culpable as the wrongdoer and that the gloss and spin of some managers belies the lies and wrongdoing they continue to carry out to further their own careers.

The Future

What will you do after everything settles down? What does the future hold for you? How do you feel? How have you coped? What have you learnt? What are the positives and negatives? What would you have done differently? And what now for your career? Is it still intact or does it lie in ruins? Is it time for a change and is this the time to reassess your life? These are big questions I know, but this could be the pivotal point you need.

And what about the wrongdoers? Where are they now? What has happened to them? Will you see them and, if so, how will you react? How do you think they will react to you? What about their friends and associates? Will you actively avoid them or go out of your way to see them? If they make conversation, what will you do? Make sure you prepare for these events – it is a bit like preparing for an interview. Visualise it and prepare some words if necessary.

Have you thought about a possible career change or at least a change in direction? What about your health? Does that need a check-up or have you spent more time on yourself as a way of coping with the stress? How has the journey impacted on your friends and family? Has it brought you closer together? Have you taken stock and reflected on who you now consider to be real friends? In adversity you see the best and the worse side of some people. Look positively on the journey and it might make you realise who is really there for you.

Have you taken up any new hobbies (such as writing a book!) or have you developed a liking for coffee mornings and now have a caffeine addiction?! Whatever happens, the future will always be bright. Brighter now that you have unburdened yourself to those who had to be told, brighter because you have helped uncover wrongdoing and brighter because you have realised your inner strength. You have helped ease the plight of another human or have made the world a safer place. Your conscience is now clear and you know you have done your bit. You are a stronger person.

Chapter 8

The End

Regardless of whether you are thinking about reporting wrongdoing, have blown the whistle, or have been through the journey, my hope is that this book has inspired you to think about making the right choice. To change things you need to do something and this book has hopefully made you realise what can be done when wrongdoing is confronted and challenged.

If you are in the middle of a dilemma as to whether to speak up, the techniques I have presented will ensure you do not become the victim. The practical tips that I have recommended will also help you through the process so that you come out the other side unscathed and a better person for it. Do not look back and be one of those who say, "I only wish that…". See this book as a form of support whenever you need it or a reference for where you are, where you are going, or where you have been so that you do not feel alone. Whether your goal is to help yourself or help others, I hope this book has helped you realise that there are others who have experienced exactly the same feelings.

Whistleblowing is a massive undertaking and is not to be underestimated. This book has hopefully enabled you to reflect, understand, and empathise with those who are taking on the challenge. It will encourage you to see whistleblowing not as a problem but the next logical step.

If you have gone through the process and come out the other side, well done. You have made a difference to your world and those of others and no-one could have asked any more of you. We salute you.

'If someone throws a stone at you throw a flower at them. But remember to throw the flowerpot with it' (Unknown)

Share It With Others

Acknowledgements

I wish to express my heart-felt thanks to all those friends and family who have supported me through the good and the more challenging times and have always been there for me. In particular Andy Sutherden (Creative Arts Agency), Nick Looby (www.feetontheground.co.uk) and Neil Barnard (www.809design.com). To my wife Heather for her seemingly endless patience, tolerance and support. To the team, thank you.

There are those who have committed wrongdoing who will never sleep well. Thank you also for having made those unfortunate enough to have met you stronger people.